SOME FAMOUS HAMLETS

SOME
FAMOUS HAMLETS

FROM

BURBAGE TO FECHTER

BY

AUSTIN BRERETON

With an Appendix

GIVING EXTRACTS FROM THE CRITICISMS ON HAMLET
BY GOETHE, COLERIDGE, SCHLEGEL, HAZLITT,
ULRICI, Etc.

Essay Index Reprint Series

BOOKS FOR LIBRARIES PRESS
FREEPORT, NEW YORK

First Published 1884

Reprinted 1972

Library of Congress Cataloging in Publication Data

Brereton, Austin, 1862-1922.
  Some famous Hamlets, from Burbage to Fechter.

  (Essay index reprint series)
  Reprint of the 1884 ed.
  CONTENTS: Richard Burbage, John Lowin, Joseph Taylor,
and Thomas Betterton.--David Garrick, John Henderson,
George Frederick Cooke.--The three Kembles, and Charles
Mayne Young. [etc,]

  1. Shakespeare, William, 1564-1616--Stage history.
2. Shakespeare, William, 1564-1616. Hamlet. 3. Actors,
English. I. Title.
PR3112.B7 1972   792'.028'0922   72-6906
ISBN 0-8369-7276-7

PRINTED IN THE UNITED STATES OF AMERICA

PREFACE.

WHEN Mr. Wilson Barrett recently announced his intention of producing "Hamlet" at the Princess's Theatre, and that he himself would represent the Prince of Denmark, no one interested in the affairs of the Drama was surprised at the announcement. At some time or other in the course of his career, it is the ambition of every actor who loves his work to appear as Hamlet. The character is so profound that every one who enacts it thinks himself capable of throwing some new light upon it, of giving to it some hitherto undiscovered meaning. An absolute failure in the part is impossible, provided that the actor be possessed of certain mere personal qualifications. But of course an actor who is more highly gifted, both intellectually and physically, than his fellow, will naturally excel in his interpretation of the character.

Since its first production, nearly three centuries ago, no play has been represented so frequently, or has given such universal satisfaction in the theatre, as " Hamlet." With Macready during his American tour, as in the time of Betterton, no piece drew so much money as Shakespeare's immortal tragedy; scarcely ten years ago, it had a run of two hundred consecutive nights in London. These facts attest its enduring popularity. It is not surprising, then, to find Mr. Wilson Barrett, who has worked his way, steadily and surely, to the front rank of the English stage, essaying for the first time before a metropolitan audience a character that has tested the genius of the greatest of actors. The revival at the Princess's Theatre will assuredly give renewed life to the play, and awaken fresh interest in the character of Hamlet: hence this volume. For, in anticipation of the production, I was tempted to see what previous representatives of Hamlet there had been, and in what manner they had interpreted the part. My theatrical library was accordingly ransacked, and from many other books I gathered together material for the formation of this one.

Those who, like myself, are familiar with the

*doings of the Stage, will find here, in an agreeable
form, I hope, what they already know. But to the
general public much contained herein will be new.
There must be many persons who are interested in
the play who have not the time or disposition to
hunt through a number of books in search of a
fact, or a date, or a reminiscence. To them, it is
hoped, this account of the most famous representatives of Hamlet in bygone days will prove accept-
able. If the book gives an hour's pleasant reading
to any one, or makes information that was previously difficult of access more easily attainable, I
shall be satisfied. The writing of it has been to
me a labour of love, and in traversing the history
of the Stage during the last three hundred years I
have spent many enjoyable hours. I can only hope
that my readers will derive as much pleasure from
the perusal of my work as I have done from the
writing of it.*

*No trouble has been spared in ascertaining the
correctness of every date given and every statement
set forth. Out of many books that have been con-
sulted, Mr. Payne Collier's "Annals of the Stage,"
and Dr. Doran's "Their Majesties' Servants,"
have been of most service to me. In the Appendix,*

extracts from the criticisms on the character of Hamlet by the most distinguished Shakespearean critics, together with a brief history of the play, are given. My account extends from Burbage to Fechter, and deals with fifteen noted Hamlets. Of living *representatives of the character—of Henry Irving in England, Edwin Booth in America, and Salvini and Rossi in Italy—I have not thought it necessary to speak in this work.* As Mr. Irving intends to appear, in the course of a few weeks, for the first time before a New York audience as Hamlet, it is hoped that this little volume may. find acceptance both in England and America.

A. B.

Queen Square, Bloomsbury.
October 1884.

CONTENTS.

—◆—

Polonius.—The best actors in the world, either for tragedy, comedy, history, pastoral, pastoral-comical, historical-pastoral, tragical-historical, tragical-comical-historical-pastoral, scene undividable, or poem unlimited : Seneca cannot be too heavy, nor Plautus too light. For the law of writ and the liberty, these are the only men.

Hamlet.—Good my lord, will you see the players well bestowed ? Do you hear, let them be well used, for they are the abstract and brief chronicles of the time : after your death you were better have a bad epitaph than their ill report while you live.

Polonius.—My lord, I will use them according to their desert.

SOME FAMOUS HAMLETS.

I.

THE first representative of Hamlet was Richard Burbage, the greatest actor of Shakespeare's time. The exact date of his birth has not been discovered, but he was probably born in, or about, the year 1566. He came of a Warwickshire family who were importantly associated with our early stage, his father being James Burbage, an actor, and the holder of theatrical property in London. Richard Burbage was on the stage, where he filled so prominent a position, before 1588, for in that year he appeared as King Gorboduc and Tereus in a dramatic piece, consisting of dumb-show and extempore dialogue, from the pen of Richard Tarlton, the most brilliant comedian of his day, and called "The Seven Deadly Sins." In 1594, he had a large share in the interests of the then newly built Globe Theatre, on the Bankside, Southwark, and he was at the head of the company performing at that house and at the Blackfriars' Theatre; that is to say, he was at the head of the tragedians, for Thomas Pope, the celebrated actor of clowns' parts, was then the leading comedian, Tarlton having died in 1588. He was the original of no less than twelve Shakespearian characters; these are Shylock, Richard III., Prince Henry, Romeo, Henry V., Brutus, Hamlet, Othello, Lear, Macbeth, Pericles, and Coriolanus. Like Garrick and Edmund Kean, he was rather short in stature, and, when "Hamlet" was produced, he had become, it would seem, somewhat corpulent. Shakespeare, apparently aware of this fact, makes the Queen allude to the defect, in the fencing scene in the last act of the tragedy :—

> *King.* Our son shall win.
> *Queen.*   He's fat and scant of breath.—
>   Here, Hamlet ; take this napkin ; rub thy brows.

From the brief records of the time that have been handed down to us, Burbage evidently was famous in Hamlet. He is undoubtedly alluded to in the following extract from "Ratsey's Ghost," an undated tract, but published some four or five years after the production of "Hamlet." Ratsey is addressing a leading actor in a company of country players: "And for you, sirrah (says he to the cheefest of them), thou hast a good presence upon the stage ; methinks thou darkenest thy merit by playing in the country ; get thee to London, for *if one man were dead*, they will have much need of men such as thou art. There would be none, in my opinion, fitter than thyself to play his parts ; my conceit is such of thee that I durst all the money in my purse upon thy head *to play Hamlet with him* for a wager." Burbage was distinguished not only in Shakespeare's plays, but in the works of the contemporary dramatists, Ben Jonson, Marlowe, Webster, Heywood, and Beaumont and Fletcher. His excellence as a tragic performer is undisputed. In his "Short Discourse of the English Stage," issued in 1664, Richard Flecknoe printed, in prose, the "description of an excellent actor." Of course Flecknoe could not have seen Burbage, but he had often heard his performances praised by those who had—a striking proof of the justly acquired fame of the actor. In his "Euterpe Restored," published in 1672, the writer put his prose of the previous eight years into verse, thus :—

THE PRAISES OF RICHARD BURBAGE

Who did appear so gracefully on the stage,
He was the admir'd example of the age,
And so observ'd all your dramatic laws,
He ne'er went off the stage but with applause;
Who his spectators and his auditors
Led in such silent chains of eyes and ears,
As none, whilst he on the stage his part did play,
Had power to speak or look another way.
Who a delightful Proteus was, and could
Transform himself into what shape he would;
And of an excellent orator had all,
In voice and gesture, we delightful call:
Who was the soul of the stage; and we may say
'Twas only he who gave life unto a play;
Which was but dead, as 'twas by the author writ,

B 2

Till he by action animated it ;
And finally he did on the stage appear
Beauty to the eye and music to the ear.
Such even the nicest critics must allow
Burbage was once ; and such Charles Hart is now.

Hart, to whom these lines were inscribed, flourished
after the Restoration. His Othello was as great as
Betterton's Hamlet; he created Alexander, was un-
matched in Brutus, and, as Doran says, his Catiline was
so unapproachable that when he died Jonson's tragedy
died with him. Rymer styles him the Æsopus, and
Mohun the Roscius, of the time. His presence charmed
the eye as his voice enchanted the ear. He was noted
for the careful study he bestowed on even the smallest
character, and when on the stage he acknowledged no
audience, but lived in his part. His salary never exceeded £3 a week, but when he became a shareholder
in the theatre he realized £1,000 a-year. He retired
from the stage in 1682 on a pension amounting to half
his salary, which, however, he had for only a year, for he
died in 1683 of a painful inward complaint, and was
buried at Stanmore Magna. There is no doubt about
Charles Hart having been a great actor. Burbage can
have been no less great for his glory to have survived
him, and for him to have been compared to Hart. Unfortunately, no evidence is at hand to prove the exact
manner in which he played Hamlet, but that he was
famous in the character is certain. Another proof of
this, if proof were needed, is to be found in an elegy

published shortly after his death, which occurred on March 13, 1618–19. The elegy is too long to be quoted in full, but some extracts from it will suffice to show how greatly Burbage was esteemed by his contemporaries.

> He's gone, and with him what a world are dead,
> Friends, every one, and what a blank instead ;
> Take him for all in all he was a man
> Not to be match'd, and no age ever can.
> No more young Hamlet, though but scant of breath,
> Shall cry "Revenge!" for his dear father's death.
>
>   *   *   *   *   *
>
> Thyself a world—the Globe thy fittest place !
> Thy stature small, but every thought and mood
> Might thoroughly from thy face be understood.
>
>   *   *   *   *   *
>
> Oft have I seen him leap into the grave,
> Suiting the person, which he seemed to have,
> Of a mad lover, with so true an eye,
> That there I would have sworn he meant to die.

In the enumeration of Burbage's list of characters the first place in the elegy is given to Hamlet. By the last extract it will be seen that he often played the character, so that he must have been noted for his acting in the part. What a pity that no Colley Cibber lived in his day to paint for us, in one of his incomparable word-pictures, *how* Burbage acted Hamlet! for the actor received his instructions direct from Shakespeare himself. But Cibber has told us how Betterton imperso-nated Hamlet, and, as we shall see presently, the traditions of Burbage's rendering were handed down to him.

Two other actors have been frequently set down as the original representatives of Hamlet; these are— John Lowin, 1576–1659, and Joseph Taylor, 1585–1653. There is really no authority for these statements. Lowin was born in the parish of St. Giles', Cripplegate, on December 9, 1576. He became a member of the company known as the King's Players in 1603, in which year he acted, with Shakespeare and six others, in the production of Ben Jonson's "Sejanus." Before the closing of the theatres in 1642, he had acquired celebrity as Falstaff, Morose, and Volpone, as Mammon, in "The Alchemist," and as Melantius, in "The Maid's Tragedy." Wright, in his "Historia Histrionica," 1699, speaks of Lowin's celebrity in these characters, but does not even mention Hamlet. On the other hand, he says that "Taylor acted Hamlet incomparably well;" but this is no authority for saying that Taylor was the first Hamlet. He could only have played it after the death of Burbage. Again, old Downes, the prompter, in his "Roscius Anglicanus," 1708, says: "In the tragedy of 'Hamlet, Prince of Denmark,' Mr. Betterton performed the part of young Hamlet. Sir William Davenant having seen Mr. Taylor, of the Black-Frier's Playhouse, act this part (who was instructed by the Author, Shakespear) remembered him so well, that he taught Mr. Betterton, in every Article; which, by his exact performance, gained the Actor Esteem and Reputation, superlative to all other players."* Now, Mr. Payne Collier, in quoting this extract in his "Annals of the Stage," has changed the name of Taylor to that of Lowin, a mistake not hitherto detected. How Mr. Collier came to adopt this error I have not been able to discover. Schlegel has also fallen into the same mistake, and he distinctly alludes to Lowin as the original Hamlet. There is no record whatever of Lowin having even so much as appeared in the character. Taylor certainly acted Hamlet, but he did so after Burbage. Taylor was also admirable as Iago, Truewit, in "The Silent Woman," and Face, in "The Alchemist." In his later days, Lowin kept an inn, "The Three Pidgeons," at Brentford.

Fortunately, the materials relative to the life of Thomas Betterton are not so scanty as those concerning the actors who appeared before the wars. The son of Charles the First's under-cook was born in Tothill Street, Westminster, in 1635. He was apprenticed to Thomas Rhodes, the bookseller, who had been wardrobe-keeper at the Blackfriars' Theatre during the reign of the King. In 1659, Rhodes obtained the first theatrical licence given after the suppression of the theatres, and gathered together a company who gave theatrical representations in the cock-pit in Drury Lane. Betterton, then only

---

* The publisher who should reprint these small, but scarce, volumes—the "Historia Histrionica" and the " Roscius Anglicanus"—would do a great service to students of the stage.

twenty-four years of age, headed the company, which also included Cave Underhill, Nokès, and Kynaston, the famous actor of women's parts.   Even then Betterton acted with success in " The Loyal Subject," " The Mad Lover," " Pericles," " The Bondman," and as Deflores in " The Changeling."   Soon after this, Sir William Davenant secured a patent from Charles II., and created Betterton and all the rest of poor Rhodes's company the King's Servants.   He opened at the Duke's Theatre, Lincoln's Inn Fields, in the spring of 1662.   Within a month after the commencement of this season, " Hamlet " was presented, with Betterton as the Prince. Betterton, be it remembered, was only twenty-seven years of age, but he electrified his audience, and for many years no play drew so much money as " Hamlet " when Betterton appeared in it, and the tragedy was frequently revived.   In proof of this, take the entry in Pepys's diary for May 28, 1663, a year after Betterton's first appearance as Hamlet : " To the Duke's House ; and there saw Hamlett done, giving us fresh reason never to think enough of Betterton."   Again, on October 31, 1668, still five years later, Pepys writes : " To the Duke of York's playhouse, and saw Hamlet, which we have not seen this year before, or more ; and mightily pleased with it, but above all with Betterton, the best part, I believe, that ever man acted."

Betterton's acting as Hamlet aroused Colley Cibber to enthusiasm.   He laments that the manner in which Betterton spoke is beyond the reach of description. " Should I therefore tell you," he says, "that all the Othellos, Hamlets, Hotspurs, Macbeths, and Brutus's, whom you may have seen from his time, have fallen far short of him, this still would give you no idea of his particular excellence. Let us see then what a particular comparison may do! whether that may yet draw him nearer to you? You have seen a Hamlet, perhaps, who, on the first appearance of his father's spirit, has thrown himself into all the straining vociferation requisite to express rage or fury, and the house has thundered with applause, tho' the misguided actor was all the while (as Shakespear terms it) tearing a passion into rags. I am the more bold to offer you this particular instance, because the late Mr. Addison, while I sat by him, to see this scene acted, made the same observation, asking me with some surprise, if I thought Hamlet should be in so violent a passion with the Ghost, which, tho' it might have astonished, it had not provoked him? for you may observe that in this beautiful speech, the passion never rises beyond an almost breathless astonishment, or an impatience, limited by filial reverence, to enquire into the suspected wrongs that may have raised him from his peaceful tomb! and a desire to know what a spirit so seemingly distrest, might wish to enjoin a sorrowful son to execute towards his future quiet in the grave? This was the light into which Betterton threw this scene : which he open'd with a pause of mute amazement ! then,

rising slowly, to a solemn, trembling voice, he made the
Ghost equally terrible to the spectator, as to himself!
and in the descriptive part of the natural emotions which
the ghastly vision gave him, the boldness of his expostu-
lation was still govern'd by decency, manly, but not
braving ; his voice never rising into that seeming outrage,
or wild defiance of what he naturally rever'd.   But, alas!
to preserve this medium, between mouthing, and meaning
too little, to keep the attention more pleasingly awake
by a temper'd spirit, than by mere vehemence of voice,
is of all the master-strokes of an actor, the most difficult to reach.   In this none yet have equall'd Betterton."

The power with which he acted the opening scene
with the Ghost must, indeed, have been great, for in the
following speech he omitted all the lines denoted by
inverted commas :—

> Angels and ministers of grace defend us !
> "Be thou a spirit of health, or goblin damn'd,
> Bring with thee airs from heaven, or blasts from hell,
> Be thy intents wicked, or charitable,
> Thou com'st in such a questionable shape,
> That I will speak to thee ! I'll call thee Hamlet,
> King, father !—Royal Dane ; O, answer me !
> Let me not burst in ignorance ! but tell,
> Why thy canoniz'd bones, hearsed in death,
> Have burst their cerements ! why the sepulchre,
> Wherein we saw thee quietly in-urn'd,
> Hath oped his ponderous and marble jaws,
> To cast thee up again ! "   What may this mean, etc.

This is an omission which I cannot trace in any other representative of Hamlet.

Addison remarked that "such an actor as Mr. Betterton ought to be recorded with the same respect as Roscius among the Romans." Only one writer, and that crabbed, disappointed Anthony Aston—sometime lawyer, then player—ever ventured to censure Betterton. But even his growls were converted into praise. When the actor was nearly seventy years of age, "Tony" Aston "could have wished that he would have resigned the part of Hamlet to some young actor who might have personated, though," observe the distinction, "he could not have acted it better ; for," he continues, "when, he threw himself at Ophelia's feet, he appeared a little too grave for a young student just returned from the University of Wittenberg. His repartees were more those of a philosopher than the sporting flashes of young Hamlet." Poor Anthony! he was a bad actor, and a critic who curiously defeated his own object. When Betterton was nearly ending his long and good life Aston complained that he had a corpulent body, that the legs and feet, swollen by gout, were large, that his eyes were small, and that he was a little pock-marked. But he was forced to admit that "his aspect was serious, venerable, and majestic," and that although his voice "was low and grumbling," yet "he could tune it by an artful climax which enforced universal attention even from the fops and orange-girls." Betterton created one

hundred and thirty characters, including Jaffier and
Valentine, three Virginiuses, and Sir John Brute. On
April 13, 1710, he took his last benefit, playing Melantius, in "The Maid's Tragedy." He was suffering
severely from gout at the time, and to enable himself to
appear he thrust his swollen foot into hot water. As a
consequence of this act the disease was forced into his
head, and the player ended a long, laborious, and
virtuous life a fortnight later.

II.

We now come to the Hamlet of the most illustrious
actor of the British stage, David Garrick (1716–1779). He
acted the character for the first time at Dublin in the
summer season of 1742, being then in the twenty-sixth
year of his age and in the first flush of his success on the
stage. His Ophelia was Peg Woffington. So great was the
excitement aroused by him in the Irish capital that the
citizens were affected with what was known as the "Garrick
fever." Here, also, he received for the first time the name
of Roscius. On returning to London he repeated his
impersonation and made another great success. Garrick,
like Betterton, made his greatest effect in the scenes with
the Ghost. When he first saw the vision, the fear with
which he seemed to be filled immediately communicated
itself to his audience. His expostulations, though warm

and imperative, were yet restrained by a filial awe. The progress of his impassioned sensation, until the Ghost beckoned him to retire, was accompanied with an admirable mixture of terror and reverence. His resolution to obey the repeated invitation, by "courteous action," of the Ghost to withdraw was determinate, but his following of the vision withal was full of awe and apprehension. When Garrick left the stage after Hamlet's first scene with the Ghost, the deafening applause of the audience continued until the impressive reappearance of the two characters. The great excellence of his Hamlet, as of all the characters he impersonated, proceeded from the manner in which he preserved the consistency of his part. His Hamlet was distinguished throughout the play by the note of filial piety struck in the first scene with the Ghost—a characteristic sign, of which the actor never lost sight. The soliloquies of Hamlet, so distinguished by their indications of the peculiar and pathetic feelings of the mind, and their varieties of sentiment, were delivered by Garrick with incomparable effect. The strong intelligence of his eye, the animated expression of his whole countenance, the flexibility of his voice, and his spirited action riveted the attention of his audience. According to his biographer, Thomas Davies, he most excelled in the speech at the end of the second act :

O, what a rogue * and peasant slave am I !

* Garrick used to say "wretch."

His final exhortation to his mother, in the closet scene, was ardent and pathetic, and excelled only in delicacy and elegance by Wilks and Spranger Barry.

Garrick's excellence in the Ghost scenes has been immortalized by Fielding in his "Tom Jones," in the chapter in which he describes the visit of the literal-minded Partridge to the playhouse. The visitor is completely taken off his guard by the truth and nature of Garrick's Hamlet, and when the Ghost, clad "in cómplete steel," appears, he shares the terrors of the "little man upon the stage," and even is so affected as to attempt a justification of his cowardice to his companion. "Nay," he says, "you may call me coward if you will; but if that little man there upon the stage is not frightened, I never saw any man frightened in my life. Ay, ay; go along with you! ay, to be sure! Who's fool then? Will you? Lud have mercy upon such foolhardiness!" But it is in the criticism of Partridge at the conclusion of the performance that the highest tribute is paid to the art of the actor: "He the best player! Why, I could act as well as he myself! I am sure, if I had seen a ghost, I should have looked in the very same manner, and done just as he did. And then, to be sure, in that scene, as you called it, between him and his mother, when you told me he acted so fine, why, Lord help me, any man—that is, any good man that had such a mother—would have done exactly the same. I know you are only joking with me; but indeed, madam, though I never was at a play

in London, yet I have seen acting before in the country ;
and the King for my money ; he speaks all his words
distinctly, half as loud again as the other. Anybody may
see *he* is an actor." No better proof of the naturalness
of the actor could be given than this. It shows how
completely he was master of that art which conceals art.
That Fielding did not exaggerate the effect of Garrick's
acting may be gathered from the anecdote related by
Macklin, and received by him from Dr. Johnson, concerning the Lichfield grocer who came to London with an
introduction to Roscius from his brother, Peter Garrick.
The man went in front of the house first, where he was,
like Partridge, completely deceived by Garrick's acting
as Abel Drugger. On the player's first appearance he
remained for some time in doubt as to whether it could
be he or not. At last, being convinced by the people
around him that it was really David whom he saw, he
felt so disgusted by the mean appearance and mercenary
conduct of the performer, which, by a foolish combination,
he attributed to the man, that he left the theatre and
went out of town without delivering the letter. On
returning to Lichfield, Peter Garrick naturally inquired
of the grocer if he had seen his brother, when he was
hesitatingly informed that the letter had never been
delivered. " To say the truth," the tradesman observed,
" I saw enough of him on the stage to make that unnecessary ; he may be rich, as I dare say any man who
lives like him must be, but "—delivering himself of a

tremendous oath—"though he is your brother, Mr. Garrick, he is one of the shabbiest, meanest, most pitiful hounds I ever saw in the whole course of my life."

An admirable description of his excellence in Hamlet is given by Hannah More : " The requisites for Hamlet are not only various, but opposed ; in him they are all united and, as it were, concentrated.   One thing I must particularly remark—that, whether in the simulation of madness, in the sinkings of despair, in the familiarity of friendship, in the whirlwind of passion, or the meltings of tenderness, he never once forgot he was a prince, and in every variety of situation and transition of feelings you discovered the highest polish of good breeding and courtly manners.   To the most eloquent expression of the eye, to the handwriting of his passions on his features, to a sensibility which tears to pieces the hearts of his auditors, to powers so unparalleled, he adds a judgement of the most exquisite accuracy, the fruit of long experience and close observation, by which he preserves every transition and gradation of the passions, keeping all under the control of a just dependence and natural consistency.   So naturally, indeed, do the ideas of the poet seem to mix with his own, that he seemed to be engaged in a succession of affecting situations ; not giving utterance to a speech, but to the instantaneous expression of his feelings, delivered in the most affecting tones of voice, and with gestures that belong only to nature. It was a fiction as delightful as fancy and as touching as truth. A few nights before, I saw him in 'Abel Drugger,' and had I not seen him in both, I should have thought it as possible for Milton to have written 'Hudibras,' and Butler ' Paradise Lost,' as for one man to have played Hamlet and Abel Drugger with such excellence."

In 1771—eight years before his death—David made some strange alterations in Shakespeare's tragedy. He considered the first act far too long, and therefore divided it into two, terminating *his* first act with Hamlet's determination to watch with Horatio and Marcellus for his father's ghost. The old third act thus became the fourth. Comparatively little change in language or scene was effected until the fifth act where, according to Shakespeare, Laertes arrives and Ophelia becomes distraught. Here the scenes in which the King and Laertes conspire to kill Hamlet were entirely changed, and the character of Laertes rendered, as Davies puts it, "more estimable." Hamlet, having escaped from Rosencrantz and Guildenstern, returns firmly resolved to be revenged for his father's death. The audience were left in ignorance of Ophelia's fate ; and the Queen, instead of being poisoned on the stage, was led from her throne and said to have become insane owing to a sense of her guilt. When Hamlet attacked the King, in the last scene, the latter drew his sword, defended himself, and was killed in the encounter. The

C

supreme genius of the actor enabled him to carry the play through despite these manipulations, but the audience objected to his expunging the Gravediggers from the play, and insisted upon these characters being restored. Osric was entirely omitted from the tragedy. Laertes was also provided with a dying speech, which gave him a slight advantage over the Prince of Denmark. No sooner was this circumstance observed than the speech was transferred to Hamlet. Garrick intended to publish this acting edition of " Hamlet," and accepted as " a compliment " from a publisher a set of Olivet's edition of Tully. But his better sense prevailed. Tully was returned, and David Garrick's " revised version " of Shakespeare's tragedy of " Hamlet " did not go through the printing-press.

A Hamlet of some note in his day was John Henderson (1747–1785), who will be better known to my readers as the Bath Roscius, and for his Falstaff. He was born in March, 1747, in Goldsmith Street, Cheapside. He made his first appearance as Hamlet, under the title of " a young gentleman," at Bath, on October 6, 1772. On the 21st of the same month we read : " Richard III., by Mr. Courtney, the young gentleman who acted Hamlet." Mr. Courtney repeated both these characters, and subsequently appeared as Benedick, Macbeth, Bobadil, Bayes, Don Felix, and Essex. His success as an actor being assured, he played Hotspur in " Henry IV." under his own name. He then acted

Fribble, Lear, Hastings, Alonzo, and Alzuma, and became an established favourite at Bath when he was only twenty-five years of age. Five years later, Colman, being in want of a novelty for the little theatre in the Haymarket, invited young Henderson, not without many misgivings, to try his fortune. He played Shylock, Hamlet, Falstaff, Leon, Don John, and Bayes, and in thirty nights he put £4,500 in the pockets of the delighted manager. In playing Shylock he challenged comparison with Macklin, and passed successfully through the ordeal. In Hamlet he had to stand against the admirers of Garrick, who found fault with the young actor for throwing away his uncle's picture subsequent to that famous speech in which Hamlet compares the portraits of his father and uncle. On the succeeding night he retained the picture in his hand, when the same party again ridiculed him, on the ground that if he was right on the first night he must perforce have been wrong on the second. He was also said not to have managed his hat properly on seeing the Ghost ; and similar complaints were made against the new actor, the exquisite music of whose voice in the words, "the fair Ophelia!" nevertheless delighted the spectators. Another disqualification, in the opinion of the Garrick worshippers, was that in his agitation in the famous closet scene he did not upset the chair as was the traditional custom. "Mr. Garrick, sir, always overthrew the chair," they said. Of some other points in Henderson's

C 2

Hamlet I shall presently speak in connection with Kemble's impersonation.

Meanwhile, it may be here noted that George Frederick Cooke (1756–1812), who excelled so greatly in other characters, failed most dismally as Hamlet. He made his first appearance in the character at Covent Garden on September 27, 1802. In his diary he says of this performance: "I acted Hamlet to a very numerous audience. Next day the newspapers, some of whom, I believe, were prepared for the business, attacked me in a manner that would have been deemed impossible to have happened to any one who had ever received the slightest approbation from an audience—a London one, I mean. I repeated it once, but never since." Five years later he writes: "I do not doubt but I had faults in abundance, but had I acted it as well as I had seen it acted by Garrick, my reception *in that character* would have been much the same." This is slightly unjust to the critics, for Cooke failed most lamentably in his attempt at what he was pleased to call Hamlet. Even the very text of the play was entirely hidden in his garbled version. Leigh Hunt, whilst recognizing his ability in characters to which he was more suited, says: "Of his Hamlet one would willingly spare the recollection. The most accomplished character on the stage is converted by him into an unpolished, obstinate, sarcastic madman."

III.

John Philip Kemble (1757–1823), the elder of the three brothers of the same name, was not only the best actor of the trio, but the most famous Hamlet. It was in this character that, on September 30, 1783, thanks to the influence of his sister, Sarah Siddons, he made his first appearance on the boards of Drury Lane Theatre. The bills announced the play to be performed as it was originally written by Shakespeare, but necessarily much of the author's text had to be omitted. The cast contained Packer as the King, Farren as Horatio, Barrymore as Laertes, Bensley as the Ghost, Baddeley as Polonius, Suett as the First Gravedigger, Mrs. Hopkins as the Queen, and Miss Field as Ophelia. The fierceness and variety of the criticism attending this performance denote that an original actor had appeared. His novel readings were commented upon, but the utmost that one critic could urge was that the actor was "too scrupulously graceful," while objection was reasonably taken to his pronouncing the word "lisp" as "lithp."

Hazlitt complained of a want of flexibility in his interpretation. "There is," he wrote, "a perpetual undulation of feeling in the character of Hamlet, but in Mr. Kemble's acting there was neither variableness nor the shadow of turning. He played it like a man in armour, with a determined inveteracy of purpose, in one undeviating straight line." But Kemble improved in his acting as he grew older, and, later on, Hazlitt found much to admire in his Hamlet : " There he was, the sweet, the graceful, the gentlemanly Hamlet. The scholar's eye shone in him with learned beauty ; the soldier's spirit decorated his person ; the beauty of his performance was its retrospective air, its intensity and abstraction ; his youth seemed delivered over to sorrow. Later actors have played the part with more energy, walked more in the sun, dashed more at effect—piqued themselves more on the girth of a foil; but Kemble's sensible, lonely Hamlet has not been surpassed." When Dr. Doran wrote, there were still alive old playgoers who told him of a grand delivery by Kemble of the soliloquies ; a mingled romance and philosophy in the whole character ; an eloquent by-play, a sweet reverence for his father, a remembrance of the *prince* with whatever companion he might be for the moment, of a beautiful affection for his mother, and of one more tender, which he could *not* conceal, for Ophelia.

On the occasion of Kemble's first appearance as Hamlet, the spectators exclaimed, " How very like his sister !" and he certainly bore a striking resemblance to the " divine Siddons." His person seemed to be finely formed, and his manners princely ; but on his brow there hung the weight of "some intolerable woe." His

Hamlet was decidedly original. He had seen no great actor whom he could have copied. His style was formed by his own taste and judgment, or, rather, grew out of his personality aided by his intellectual habits. He was naturally solemn and deliberate in his nature ; his walk was always slow, and his expression of countenance contemplative ; his utterance, for the most part, was somewhat tardy, although always finely articulate, and seemed to proceed rather from organization than voice. In almost every scene of " Hamlet " there were points in the dialogue that caused the delivery of the young actor to be contrasted with that of Garrick or Henderson. These points were noted at the time by Boaden. The first objection was to an emphasis. Kemble was instructed to say—

> 'Tis an *un*-weeded garden that grows to seed.

But he considered that " un-weeded " was quite as intelligible with the usual accent as the unusual one. He was the first representative of Hamlet who, after having recognized Horatio and Marcellus by name, turned courteously towards Bernado and applied the " Good even, sir," to him. It was observed how keenly he inserted an insinuation of the King's intemperance at the words—

> We'll teach you to drink *deep* ere you depart.

He restored to the stage " *dearest* foe " and " *beteeme* the winds of heaven." When told of his father's

ghost he was overcome with a flood of tenderness, and
it was with tears that he murmured—

> He was a man, take him for all in all,
> I shall not look upon his like again.

Professor Richardson terms

> My father,—methinks I see my father,

the "most solemn and striking apostrophe that ever
poet invented," and by Kemble's treatment it certainly
became so.   In the line

> Did you not speak to it?

he turned towards Horatio and addressed the "you"
particularly to him, speaking emphatically, but tenderly.
He submitted this emphasis to the judgment of Dr.
Johnson.   "To be sure, sir," said Johnson, "'*you*'
should be strongly marked. I told Garrick so long
since, but Davy never could see it."   In the lines,

> And for my soul, what can it do to that,
> Being a thing immortal as itself?

Garrick laid great stress upon "that," but Kemble used
to give the line thus—

> And for my soul, what CAN it do to *that?*

It is worthy of note that, according to Boaden, Kemble, not Kean,* was the first Hamlet who, in ad-

---

* Writing in March, 1817, of Kean's Hamlet, Hazlitt said : "Mr. Kean
introduced in this part a *new reading*, as it is called, which we think perfectly
correct. In the scene where he breaks from his friends at the command of his

dressing the Ghost, having drawn his sword at the words—

> By heaven I'll make a ghost of him that lets me,

retained it in his right hand, but turned his left toward the spirit, dropping the weapon after him—a tasteful and judicious change. All previous Hamlets had pointed the sword toward the Ghost. Kemble also knelt at the descent of the Ghost—an innovation that was immediately adopted by Henderson. In the scene with Polonius, where Hamlet is asked what he reads, and answers, "Slanders, sir, slanders," Kemble, in order to give better expression to his wildness, tore the leaf from the book. Garrick pronounced "The mobled queen" after the player as in doubt; Kemble, as in sympathy. Garrick used to say to Horatio,

> Aye, in my heart of *heart*, as I do thee,

but Kemble and Henderson agreed in saying " heart *of* heart." Both these actors gave

> The croaking raven doth bellow for revenge

as a reflection of their own case, in contrast to Garrick, who addressed the words to Lucianus. In the closet

---

father, he keeps his sword pointed behind him, to prevent them following him, instead of holding it before him to protect him from the Ghost." Boaden's " Life of Kemble," was published in 1825, so that it appears that the biographer attributed to his hero one of Kean's original effects. This point has been adopted by all successive Hamlets.

scene, Kemble addressed the "Is it the King?" to the universe rather than to the Queen, the better to mark his filial devotion; and his performance in this scene was objected to because he was so tender to his mother! In the churchyard scene he was too studiously graceful and too cold to be effective, and the audience missed the deep pathos of Henderson's

What! the fair Ophelia!

In fencing with Laertes he was eminently graceful, and his studied death scene brought a scholarly, intellectual impersonation to a close. It may be noted that he played Hamlet in a modern court dress of rich black velvet, with a star on the breast, the garter and pendant riband of an order, deep ruffles, a mourning sword and buckles, and with the hair in powder.

Stephen Kemble (1758–1822) did not acquire much celebrity on the stage, nor was his Hamlet of any consequence, but his name may be recorded here. He was born in 1758, on the night that his mother played Anne Boleyn. He left a chemist's shop for the stage. His theatrical career may be said to have commenced in Dublin, where he was speedily extinguished by the success of his brother, John Philip. He appeared at Covent Garden, in 1783, as Othello, to the Desdemona of Miss Satchell, whom he afterwards married. After subsequently playing old men at the Haymarket, he opened a theatre in Edinburgh, which, however, did not bring him a fortune. In 1803, he appeared at Drury Lane as Falstaff, a character which his remarkable obesity enabled him to play without padding. He did not act the character by any means badly, but his performance could not sweep the recollection of Henderson from the memory of the elder playgoers. After another disappearance from the metropolis, he returned, played a few characters to which his size suited him, and, in 1818, opened Drury under his own management, introducing his son Henry from Bath in the character of Romeo. The following year the theatre was let to Robert William Elliston. Stephen withdrew into private life, and died in 1822. He played Hamlet for his benefit occasionally. He dressed the character in an old-fashioned black coat, breeches, vest, shoes, buckles, and a large, flowing auburn wig. More than once the lines,

> O, that this too, too solid flesh would melt,
> Thaw, and resolve itself into a dew,

provoked the smiles of the audience. Stephen Kemble gave no new light to the character, nor was he particularly brilliant in it. He was, no doubt, induced to appear in the part because of the success of his wife as Ophelia. She was a delightful actress, and her clear, silver voice, " most musical, most melancholy," drew tears from all who witnessed her mad scene in " Hamlet."

Charles Kemble (1775–1854), the youngest of the three

brothers, was born at Brecknock, and, like his brother,
John, educated at Douai. When only seventeen years of
age he abandoned the Post-office for the stage, making
his first appearance at Sheffield, as Orlando. Two
years later—that is, on April 21, 1794—he made his first
appearance in London (on the opening of new Drury
Lane Theatre, the house built by Holland, and burned
in 1809) as Malcolm to the Macbeth of John Kemble
and the Lady Macbeth of Mrs. Siddons. He was
intelligent, but awkward in action, ungraceful in deport-
ment, and the weakness of his voice was always against
him. He "gradually," says Doran, " became one of the
most graceful and refined of actors. He was enabled to
seize upon a domain of comedy which his brother and
sister could never enter with safety to their fame. In his
hands, secondary parts soon assumed a more than
ordinary importance from the finish with which he
acted them. His Laertes was as carefully played as
Hamlet, and there was no other Cassio but his while
he lived, nor any Falconbridge, then or since, that could
compare with his ; and in Macduff, Charles Kemble had
no rival. In the tender or witty lover, the heroic soldier,
or the rake who is nevertheless a gentleman, he was the
most distinguished player of his time." Mrs. Siddons
considered that his Hamlet was fine in conception, but
inferior in execution to his brother's. In tragic parts
his enunciation was always very measured, and in the
play of the features the actor was ever present. This

was particularly noted in Hamlet, in which his assumed seriousness made his long face appear so much longer than ordinary that in the rebuke to his mother his eyebrows seemed to vanish beneath his wig while his chin disappeared into his waistcoat.

From the description of his Hamlet given by his daughter, Fanny, it appears that Charles Kemble made his greatest hit in the scene with Ophelia:— " The great beauty of all my father's performances, but particularly of Hamlet, is a wonderful accuracy in the detail of the character which he represents—an accuracy which modulates the emphasis of every word, the nature of every gesture, the expression of every look, and which renders the whole a most laborious and minute study. My father possesses certain physical defects—a faintness of colouring in the face and eye, a weakness of voice ; and the corresponding intellectual deficiencies—a want of intensity, vigour, and concentrating power. . . . I have acted Ophelia three times with my father, and each time, in that beautiful scene where his madness and his love gush forth together like a torrent swollen with storms, that bears a thousand blossoms on its troubled waters, I have experienced such deep emotion as hardly to be able to speak. The exquisite tenderness of his voice, the wild compassion and forlorn pity of his looks, bestowing that on others which, of all others, he most needed ; the melancholy restlessness, the bitter self-scorning ; every shadow of expression and intonation was so full of the mingled anguish that the human heart is capable of enduring, that my eyes scarce fixed on his ere they were filled with tears ; and long before the scene was over, the letters and jewel-cases I was tendering to him were wet with them. The hardness of professed actors and actresses is something amazing. After this part, I could not but recall the various Ophelias I have seen, and commend them for the astonishing absence of everything like feeling which they exhibited. Oh, it made my heart sore to act it." It may not be out of place to note that Charles Kemble's wife, Maria Theresa de Camp, was the original Lady Elizabeth Freelove, in a piece of her own writing, " The Day after the Wedding," which still survives.

Another famous Hamlet of this period was Charles Mayne Young (1777–1856). He was born in Fenchurch Street, and was the son of a surgeon. While yet a child he won the affections of the King and Queen during a short visit to Copenhagen. His education was commenced at Eton, but the dissipation of his father rendered it necessary for him to be sent to the Merchant Taylors' School. The conduct of the father became so bad that, when comparative boys, Charles and his brother removed their mother from the paternal roof and undertook her support. Charles commenced life as a merchant's clerk, but speedily left the desk for the stage. He made his *début* in 1798 at Liverpool, as Young Norval, under the name of Mr. Green. He became successful immediately, and won an established position in Manchester. In 1807, a correspondence was opened between him and Colman relative to an engagement at the Haymarket Theatre. Young asked for £20 a-week and a benefit, to which the manager replied that such terms "much exceeded any bargain formed within my memory between a manager of the Haymarket Theatre and a performer coming to try his fortunes upon the London boards." "We propose, then," he says, "£14 a-week and a benefit, you to take all the profits of that benefit, however great, after paying the established charges. Should there be a deficiency, we ensure that you should clear £100 by it. This, upon mature deliberation, is all we think prudence enables us to offer." Under these terms Young came to London. He made his first appearance at the Haymarket on June 22, 1807, as Hamlet. He made an instantaneous success, and Hamlet remained to the end his most popular impersonation. It was in this character that at Covent Garden, on May 30, 1832, he took his final leave of the stage ; the receipts on the occasion amounted to £643, and £81 were returned to persons who were unable to find even standing room.

Young belonged to the Kemble school, but he had more natural feeling and fire than the Kembles. "I cannot help thinking," says the Vicomte de Soligny, "what a sensation Young would have created had he belonged to the French instead of to

the English stage.   With a voice almost as powerful
rich, and sonorous as that of Talma ; action more free
flowing, graceful, and various ; a more expressive face
and a better person ; he would have been hardly second
in favour and attraction to that greatest of living actors
As it is, he admirably fills up that place in the English
stage which would have been a blank without him."
During his first performance of Hamlet in London,
Young was unnerved by the sound of a persistent hiss.
The frowning man who hissed so vehemently turned out
to be his father !   But, despite the malignant hissing,
Young triumphed, and his Hamlet became the talk of
the town.   His great hits were made in the play scene,
and in the fencing scene in the last act, where his nature
was better suited than in the scenes with Ophelia and
his mother.   These lacked tenderness, and were given
with a great show of irritability that was bad in contrast to the pathos and tenderness of previous Hamlets
in them.   And the lines, " Ah ! who would fardels
bear ? "—" Give me the man that is not passion's slave ! "
—" What a piece of work is man ! " were delivered with
undue passion and warmth.   Young's Hamlet was fiery
and impetuous, but Charles Mayne held his ground in
the character during the twenty-five years he was on the
London stage.   When he retired, Mathews played
Polonius, and Macready the Ghost, to his Hamlet.

IV.

Edmund Kean (1787–1833) played Hamlet at Drury
Lane for the first time on March 12, 1814, two months
fter he had electrified the audience by his Shylock and
aved the theatre from ruin. He always considered
Hamlet one of his best impersonations, but it was not
o fine a performance as his Othello, Shylock, or his
ago. Tenderness to Ophelia, affection for his mother,
everential awe of his father's spirit, and a fixed resolu-
ion to fulfil the mission accorded to him by that spirit;
vere the prominent motives of his Hamlet. His grace
and earnestness throughout, and the tender vibration of
his voice when speaking to the Ghost, were specially
noted. Mrs. Garrick took such interest in his performance that she induced him to alter his reading of the
closet scene. Kean played this with an infinite tenderness, but "Davy," as Mrs. Garrick always called her
deceased husband when speaking of him to an intimate
friend, was rather severe in his treatment of the Queen.
Kean adopted the old lady's well-meant suggestion, but
the new reading went against his convictions, and, after
two or three nights, he played the scene, as he had
previously done, with marvellous tenderness. An original
point in his acting of Hamlet has become stage
property. This is in the scene with Ophelia, at the

D

close of which Kean used to return from the very extremity of the stage, take Ophelia's hand, kiss it with tender rapture, look mournfully upon her, with eyes full of beautiful significance, and then rush off the stage. This was a fine effect that never failed, and always secured the tumultuous applause of the house. The nature, without vulgarity or affectation, which he invariably displayed throughout the part, struck home to the feelings of every spectator.

"High as Mr. Kean stood in our opinion before," wrote Hazlitt of Kean's Hamlet, "we have no hesitation in saying that he stands higher in it from the powers displayed by this last effort. If it was less perfect as a whole, there were parts in it of a higher cast of excellence than any part of his Richard." But the critic considered his general delineation of the character wrong. It was too strong and pointed. There was often a severity, approaching to virulence, in the common observations and answers. "There is nothing of this," continues Hazlitt, "in Hamlet. He is, as it were, wrapped up in the cloud of his reflections, and only *thinks aloud*. There should, therefore, be no attempt to impress what he says upon others by any exaggeration of emphasis or manner; no talking *at* his hearers. There should be as much of the gentleman and scholar as possible infused into the part, and as little of the actor. A pensive air of sadness should sit unwilling upon his brow, but no appearance of fixed and sullen gloom.

He is full of 'weakness and melancholy,' but there is
no harshness in his nature. Hamlet should be the most
amiable of misanthropes. There is no one line in this
play that should be spoken like any one line in Richard ;
yet Mr. Kean did not appear to us to keep the two
characters always distinct. He was least happy in the
last scene with Guildenstern and Rosencrantz. In some
of these more familiar scenes he displayed more energy
than was requisite ; and in others, where it would have
been appropriate, did not rise equal to the exigency of
the occasion. In particular, the scene with Laertes,
where he leaps into the grave, and utters the exclama-
tion, ''Tis I, Hamlet the Dane !' had not the tumultuous and overpowering effect we expected from it.
To point out the defects of Mr. Kean's performance of
the part is a less grateful but a much shorter task than
to enumerate the many striking beauties which he gave
to it, both by the power of his action and the true feeling of nature. His surprise when he first sees the
Ghost, his eagerness and filial confidence in following
it, the impressive pathos of his action and voice in
addressing it, ' I'll call thee Hamlet, *Father*, Royal
Dane,' were admirable. . . . . The manner of his taking
Guildenstern and Rosencrantz under each arm, under
pretence of communicating his secret to them, when he
only means to trifle with them, had the finest effect, and
was, we conceive, exactly in the spirit of the character.
So was the suppressed tone of irony in which he ridicules

those who gave ducats for his uncle's picture, though they would 'make mouths at him' while his father lived.   Whether the way in which Mr. Kean hesitates in repeating the first line of the speech in the interview with the player, and then, after several ineffectual attempts to recollect it, suddenly hurries on with it, 'The rugged Pyrrhus, etc.,' is in perfect keeping, we have some doubts ; but there was great ingenuity in the thought, and the spirit and life of the execution was beyond everything.   Hamlet's speech in describing his own melancholy, his instructions to the players, and the soliloquy on death were all delivered by Mr. Kean in a tone of fine, clear, and natural recitation."   Hazlitt considered his kissing of Ophelia's hand "the finest commentary that was ever made on Shakespeare.   It explained the character at once (as he meant it) as one of disappointed hope, of bitter regret, of affection suspended, and not obliterated, by the distractions of the scene around him.   The manner in which Mr. Kean acted in the scene of the play before the king and queen was the most daring of any, and the force and animation which he gave to it cannot be too highly applauded.   Its extreme boldness bordered 'on the verge of all we hate,' and the effect it produced was a test of the extraordinary powers of this extraordinary actor."

William Charles Macready (1793-1873) appeared for the first time as Hamlet at Newcastle in 1811, being then only eighteen years of age. He was naturally nervous on the occasion, but he succeeded beyond his hopes, and frequently repeated the performance at other provincial theatres. He represented Hamlet for the first time in London at Covent Garden on June 8, 1821. Macready gave it as his opinion that " no actor possessed of moderate advantages of person, occasional animation, and some knowledge of stage business can entirely fail in the part of Hamlet." He continued studying the character until the close of his long career, and even then was dissatisfied with his interpretation. To act the part was always a source of delight to him, and in America no play drew so much money as " Hamlet " when he appeared in it. To use his exact words, " ' Hamlet ' has brought me more money than any play in America." During his visit to New York, Macready recorded that he lay on his sofa at the hotel, "ruminating upon the play of ' Hamlet '; upon the divine spirit which God lent to that man, Shakespeare, to create such intellectual realities full of beauty and power, inheriting the ordinary wickednesses of humanity, the means of attracting so strongly the affections and wonder of men. It seems to me," he added on this occasion, " as if only now, at fifty-one years of age, I thoroughly see and appreciate the artistic power of Shakespeare in this great human phenomenon." Macready was a thorough artist, very conscientious, greatly in earnest, and very careful about all the re-

sources of his art.   His voice was powerful and extensive
in compass, and capable of delicate modulation in quiet
passages, though with a tendency to scream in violent
ones.   According to George Henry Lewes, his voice
possessed "tones that thrilled, and tones that stirred
tears.   His declamation was mannered and unmusical ;
yet his intelligence always made him follow the winding
meanings through the involutions of the verse, and never
allowed you to feel that he was speaking words which he
did not understand."   His person was good and his face
expressive.   His Hamlet was studied and correct, according to his own comprehension of the character, but
his portrayal of it was monotonous, harsh, and severe.
In those parts of the play where action and passion are
appropriate, he succeeded ; but in the more subtle and
refined passages he was cold and uninteresting.   His
greatest hit was made in the play scene, which he always
acted with power, and he did not fail in making a striking effect in the scenes with the Ghost.   But he scolded
Ophelia and ranted at his mother.   He made no good
impression by his delivery of the soliloquies ; as rendered by him they were the mere cold declamations of
the practised elocutionist.   Mr. Lewes, whilst making
due allowance for the intelligence which his impersonation displayed, was of opinion that his Hamlet was
absolutely bad.   " He was lachrymose and fretful ; too
fond of a cambric pocket-handkerchief to be really
affecting, nor, as it seemed to me, had he that sympathy

with the character which would have given an impressive unity to his performance ; it was 'a thing of shreds and patches,' not a whole." Thus it will be seen that a great critic thought Macready's Hamlet bad, and had no hesitation in saying so, yet, to repeat the actor's words once again, "' Hamlet' has brought me more money than any play in America," and therein was reward !

Junius Brutus Booth (1796–1852) was born in London, in the parish of St. Pancras, on May 1, 1796. He received a classical education, and early in life evinced a decided capacity for drawing and literature. He learned printing, and for a time remained in the office of his father, a lawyer, where he was employed in copying legal documents. Resolving to become an actor, he left his home against the wishes of his father, and commenced his stage career at Deptford, on December 13, 1813, as Campillo in " The Honeymoon," at a salary of twenty shillings a-week. He passed his probation principally at the Brighton and Worthing theatres, and on February 12, 1817, appeared at Covent Garden as Richard III. But he was unable to contend against the superior genius of Edmund Kean, then in the full tide of his success at Drury Lane, and after a short, sharp struggle, Booth left England for America, where he firmly established himself. He died on board the *J. S. Chenoweth*, on the voyage from New Orleans to Cincinnati, on November 30, 1852. I can find no record of his having appeared as Hamlet in

London, but he frequently acted it for his benefit in
America. His Hamlet had many beauties and some
defects. He possessed many physical advantages for
the character. In his youth, his figure, from the waist
upwards, was perfect : the chest massive but not heavy,
the head firmly set, and the face often lit up with a
singular spiritual beauty, the grey eyes being alternately
filled with fire, intelligence, and splendour, and, anon, with
the most fascinating, dreamy softness. But against
these beauties of person he had the disadvantage of
coarse and awkwardly-shaped limbs—a defect that
frequently spoilt his best assumptions. In Hamlet,
where there are so many scenes of repose, this defect
was the more glaring, but even then his magnetism
won the entire attention of his audience. With his
voice he could express tenderness, terror, anger, or
carcasm, at will. This gift, so indispensable to a perfect rendering of Hamlet, he often neglected altogether,
and never took full advantage of it. He hurried care-
lessly over the soliloquies, impatient to reach the point
at which, by some rapid action or passionate gesture,
or the delivery of a single word, he could powerfully
impress his audience. This fault was the less excusable
as Booth was an accomplished scholar and an elocutionist
of rare and surpassing excellence, unlike Kean, who
was comparatively uneducated, and had little or no
power of elocution unless he was fired by some strong
emotion, when the music of his voice moved all

hearers. "His splendour," writes an authoritative critic, " was most irregular. Although, no doubt, his performance, as a whole, was pre-arranged in his mind and regulated, as all matters of art which hope to endure must be, he still trusted, to a great extent, for the carrying out of his effects, to the impulse of the moment. He had, consequently, like all men of this class, his moments of inspiration. There were times when the auditor, following him through Hamlet, would have to travel for hours over a flat, level, and murky waste, waiting for some touch of grandeur to relieve the desolate evenness, when suddenly would come across the gloom a flash which, though you cried, Behold it, it was gone—a flash of genius that electrified the audience, and burned its mark on every memory. On other nights, when in the mood, his splendour would be sustained, and all the lovely lights and shades of Hamlet's character, the profound and over-wrought sensibility—the moody waywardness of temper, whose sadness breaks off into melancholy mirthfulness, where the passionate outbursts of indignation and grief lapse into idle speculation—would find a most exquisite interpretation. In the passages of tenderness, and in those in which Hamlet, overcome with the forlorn sense of desolation, and bewildered with all that is going on around him, and his own peculiar relation to it, contemplates closing his existence, Booth found his greatest excellence. He seemed to linger with special love on those velvety spots of tenderness, as in the scene with Ophelia, with which Shakespeare delights to relieve his landscape. In the expression of passion he was superb. At times, so possessed was he with the spirit and influence of the power he would portray that, in his eagerness, he clutched the passion by the blade, and terrified the audience with the gash. He had the rare art of discovering the most subtle changes of feeling, and of marking those slight variations of expression which take place on the turn of a thought or the impulse of a fancy. No other actor, perhaps, has produced so all-powerful and overwhelming an impression by a single word or look. In the utterance of a word, in a sudden look, Mr. Booth has thrilled his audience with awe, and realized the very height of that intensity which is the greatest characteristic of genius. Mr. Booth, like Mr. Kean, was also a master of all those external accomplishments which could serve to beautify his art, and the grace and elegance with which he played his part in the passage of arms in Hamlet might well challenge the compliments and admiration of the King."

V.

Charles John Kean (1811–1868), born at Waterford on January 18, 1811, had to wait twenty-seven years before he could obtain a suitable opportunity of impersonating Hamlet on the London stage. On January 8, 1838, he commenced an engagement of twenty nights at Drury Lane, at a salary of fifty pounds a-night. He appeared as Hamlet, and was so successful that he repeated the performance for three weeks, his engagement being naturally extended beyond the limits originally prescribed. His Hamlet was at least a careful, polished, and efficient performance. As a whole, it was considered a striking, energetic, skilful interpretation, undeformed by any such marked blemish as would mar the general good effect it created. But he was too lachrymose, and the extreme slowness of his enunciation threatened, on more than one occasion, to wreck the performance. His delivery of the soliloquies was painfully slow, and some of his pauses were so prolonged that the point of the sentence was lost. Of course his scene with the Ghost was effective, but his intelligence was not prominently marked until after his interview with the spirit, when his manner of talking to his friends was admirable. But he made no impression in the famous soliloquy beginning " To be, or not to be," and that passage commencing " I am myself indifferent honest " was spoken so rapidly that it was quite impossible for the audience to follow his words. In the play scene, however, he succeeded in forcibly affecting spectators by the burst of exultation when Hamlet discovers the guilt of the King. Strange to say, Charles Kean's greatest effect in Hamlet was created by his

Is it the King ?

in the closet scene when Hamlet has killed Polonius. The voice of anxious inquiry, the attitude, the depth of eager expression with which he endowed this passage were extremely effective. He fenced with consummate skill, but his death scene was needlessly protracted and unnecessarily painful. His Hamlet appears to have been a melodramatic performance rather than a Shakespearean one. Nor did he throw any new light upon the character, or the play. Mr. G. H. Lewes does not specially allude to Charles Kean's impersonation of Hamlet, but no doubt he had that amongst the other Shakespearean performances of the actor in his mind when he wrote " he has added nothing to the elucidation of the characters ; he has given no fresh light to players or public ; but he has greatly improved the scenic representation, and has lavished time and money on the archæological illustration of the plays. He has striven for public applause by appealing to the public taste ; and he has gained that applause."

The career of Charles Albert Fechter (1823–1879) will no doubt be still fresh in the recollection of many of my readers. It may be noted that he made his *début* at the Princess's Theatre on October 27, 1860, as Ruy Blas. Six weeks later—that is to say, on March 20, 1861—he appeared for the first time as Hamlet. Unfortunately I had no opportunity of witnessing Fechter's Hamlet. I am therefore constrained to quote from those who had that advantage. Ample record of the naturalness and beauty of this imper- sonation has been placed on record. "Perhaps," wrote Charles Dickens, " no innovation in art was ever accepted with so much favour by so many intelligent persons pre-committed to, and pre-occupied by, another system as Mr. Fechter's Hamlet. I take this to have been the case (as it unquestionably was in London), not because of its picturesqueness; not because of its novelty; not because of its many scattered beauties ; but because of its perfect consistency with itself. Its great and satisfying originality was in its possessing the merit of a distinctly conceived and executed idea. Mr. Fechter's Hamlet—a pale, woe-begone Norseman, with long flaxen hair, wearing a strange garb never associated with the part upon the English stage (if ever seen there at all), and making a piratical swoop upon the whole fleet of little theatrical prescriptions without meaning, or, like Dr. Johnson's celebrated friend, with only one idea in them, and that a wrong one—never could have achieved its extraordinary success but for its animation by one pervading purpose to which all changes were made intelligently subservient." Fechter's Hamlet was marked in some passages by exquisite beauty of thought and

expression, and, as a whole, by high refinement and
excellent taste. In all the lighter scenes he played with
the ease and spirit of a typical French actor. But he
interested rather than moved his audience. He gave
undue prominence to the meditative element in Hamlet's nature, concerning himself chiefly with the play
of intellect revealed in the soliloquies. The more
passionate scenes were neglected by him. "The merits
and deficiencies of Mr. Fechter," wrote Mr. Oxenford,
"cannot be better illustrated than by the fact that the
play scene and the closet scene are those with which he
produces least effect, whereas in the second act he
makes a most powerful impression"—a very significant
fact. The various technicalities of his rendering have
been summed up by Mr. Dutton Cook: "It was the
firm belief of Fechter's Hamlet, in defiance of general
opinion to the contrary, that Queen Gertrude was
Claudius's accomplice in the murder of her husband.
In the time of Fechter's Hamlet it was the fashion in
Denmark to wear a medallion portrait, swinging from a
gold chain, round the neck. Fechter's Hamlet wore thus
a portrait of his father; the Queen wore a portrait of
Claudius; Guildenstern was similarly adorned. Usually
there is not a pin to choose between Rosencrantz and
Guildenstern; the unfortunate gentlemen are alike
odious to Hamlet, and they are slaughtered off the stage,
at the instigation of that prince, after they have been
well murdered in the presence of the house by their
histrionic representatives. But to Fechter's Hamlet,

Rosencrantz was less hateful than Guildenstern : Rosencrantz wore no portrait around his neck. When
Fechter's Hamlet spoke his first speech, and compared
the late King to Hyperion, and Claudius to a satyr, he
produced and gazed fondly at his father's picture ; when
he mentioned his uncle's 'picture in little,' he illustrated
his meaning by handling the medallion worn by Guildenstern ; in the closet scene he placed his miniature
of his father side by side with his mother's miniature of
Claudius ; when, at the close of their interview, Gertrude
outstretched her arm, and would embrace her son, he
held up sternly the portrait of his father ; the wretched
woman recoiled and staggered from the stage, and
Hamlet reverentially kissed the picture as he murmured,
' I must be cruel to be kind.' In the play scene, Fechter's Hamlet, when he rose at the discomfiture of
Claudius, tore the leaves from the play-book and flung
them in the air ; in the scene with Ophelia, Fechter's
Hamlet did not perceive that the King was watching
him ; had he known *that*, he would have been so convinced of his uncle's guilt that the play would have
been unnecessary. In the fourth act, if Fechter's Hamlet had not been well guarded, he would have killed the
King then and there. In the last scene, a gallery ran at
the back of the stage, with short flights of stairs on
either side, all exits and entrances being made by means
of these stairs. Upon the confession of Laertes, the
King endeavoured to escape up the right-hand staircase.
Hamlet, perceiving this, rushed up the left-hand stairs,

and, encountering Claudius in the centre of the gallery, there dispatched him."

According to George Henry Lewes, Fechter gave a new and charming representation of the part. On leaving the theatre, after "Hamlet," Mr. Lewes was convinced that his interpretation was one of the very best he had seen. His physique enabled him to represent Hamlet, and his naturalism was artistic. " His Hamlet," continued this critic, " was ' natural,' but this was not owing to the simple fact of its being more conversational and less stilted than usual. If Shakespeare's grandest language seemed to issue naturally from Fechter's lips, and did not strike you as out of place, which it so often does when mouthed on the stage, the reason was that he formed a tolerably true conception of Hamlet's nature, and could *represent* that conception. It was his personality which enabled him to represent that conception. . . . . Intellectually and physically he so satisfies the audience that they exclaim, ' How natural !' Hamlet is fat, according to his mother's testimony; but he is also— at least in Ophelia's eyes—very handsome—

> The courtier's, soldier's, scholar's eye, tongue, sword,
> The glass of fashion, and the mould of form,
> The observed of all observers.

Fechter is lymphatic, delicate, handsome, and, with his long, flaxen curls, quivering, sensitive nostrils, fine eye, and sympathetic voice, perfectly represents the graceful prince. His aspect and bearing are such that the eye rests on him with delight. Our sympathies are completely secured. All those scenes which demand the qualities of an accomplished comedian he plays to perfection. Seldom have the scenes with the players, with Polonius, with Horatio, with Rosencrantz or Guildenstern, or the quieter monologues, been better played; they are touched with so cunning a grace, and a manner so *natural*, that the effect is delightful. We do not feel, in the presence of an individual, a character, but feel that the individual is consonant with our previous conception of Hamlet, and with the part assigned him in the play. The passages of *emotion* are also rendered with some sensibility. His delightful and sympathetic voice, and the unforced fervour of his expression, triumph over the foreigner's accent and the foreigner's mistakes in emphasis. This is really a considerable triumph; for, although Fechter pronounces English very well for a Frenchman, it is certain that his accent greatly interferes with the due effect of his speeches. But the foreign accent is as nothing compared with the frequent errors of emphasis; and *this* surely might be overcome by diligent study, if he would consent to submit to the rigorous criticism of some English friend who would correct him every time he errs. The sense is often perturbed, and sometimes violated, by this fault. Yet so great is the power of true emotion that

E

even *this* is forgotten directly he touches the feelings of
the audience, and in his great speech,

> O ! what a rogue and peasant slave am I !

no one hears the foreigner.   Physically, then, we may
say that his Hamlet is perfectly satisfactory ; nor is it
intellectually open to more criticism than must always
arise in the case of a character which admits of so many
readings.   It is certainly a fine conception, consonant
in general with what the text of Shakespeare indicates.
It is the nearest approach that I have seen to the reali-
zation of Goethe's idea expounded in the celebrated
critique, in 'Wilhelm Meister,' that there is a burden
laid on Hamlet too heavy for his soul to bear.   The
refinement, the feminine delicacy, the vacillation of
Hamlet are admirably represented ; and it is only in
the more tragic scenes that we feel any shortcoming.
For these scenes he wants the tragedian's personality ;
and once for all let me say that by personality I do not
simply mean the qualities of voice and person, but the
qualities which give the force of animal passion de-
manded by tragedy, and which cannot be represented
except by a certain animal power."   The account of
Fechter's Hamlet brings this work to a close.

It is we *who are Hamlet.*—HAZLITT.

———✦———

Flame trembles most when it doth highest rise.—DAVENANT.

———✦———

Gervinus remarks, that whenever the name of Shakespeare is mentioned, the play of Hamlet first comes to remembrance.
DR. CONOLLY.

———✦———

Shakespeare is a being of a higher nature, to whom I do but look up, and whom it is my part to worship and to honour.—GOETHE.

———✦———

Oh weary life ! oh weary death !
Oh spirit and heart made desolate !
Oh damnèd vacillating state.—TENNYSON.

———✦———

We have here an oak planted in a costly vase, fit only to receive lovely flowers within its bosom; the roots expand, the vase is shattered.—GOETHE.

Take up any Shakespeare you will, from the first collection of his works to the last, which has been read, *and look what play bears the most obvious signs of perusal. My life for it, they will be found in the volume which contains the play of " Hamlet."*—JOHN PHILIP KEMBLE.

———◆———

> *Self-disgust*
> *Gnaws at the roots of being, and doth hang*
> *A heavy sickness on the beams of day.*
> *Cursèd ! accursèd be the freaks of nature,*
> *That mar us from ourselves.*—HORNE.

———◆———

He has the desire and the power to accomplish great things, but it must be in obedience to the dictates of his own thoughts, and by his own independent, original, creative energy. . . . . The poor plans and intentions of man do not miscarry through the weakness of their authors, but their baseless projects are also, by an intrinsic necessity, as frequently crossed and frustrated by the equally baseless empire of chance.—ULRICI.

———◆———

Hamlet's character is the prevalence of the abstracting and generalizing habit over the practical. He does not want courage, skill, will, or opportunity ; but every incident sets him thinking ; and it is curious, and at the same time strictly natural, that Hamlet, who all the play seems reason itself, should be impelled at last, by mere accident, to effect his object. I have a smack of Hamlet myself, if I may say so.—COLERIDGE.

APPENDIX.

———◦•◦———

SOFT and from a noble stem, this royal flower had sprung up under the immediate influences of majesty; the idea of moral rectitude with that of princely elevation, the feeling of the good and dignified with the consciousness of high birth, had in him been unfolded simultaneously. He was a prince, by birth a prince; and he wished to reign, only that good men might be good without obstruction. Pleasing in form, polished by nature, courteous from the heart, he was meant to be the pattern of youth and the joy of the world.

Without any prominent passion, his love for Ophelia was a still presentiment of sweet wants. His zeal in knightly accomplishments was not entirely his own; it needed to be quickened and inflamed by praise bestowed on others for excelling in them. Pure in sentiment, he knew the honourable-minded, and could prize the rest which an upright spirit tastes on the bosom of a friend. To a certain degree, he had learned to discern and value the good and the beautiful in arts and sciences: the mean, the vulgar, was offensive to him; and if hatred could take root in his tender soul, it was only so far as to make him properly despise the false and changeful insects of a court, and play with them in easy scorn. He was calm in his temper, artless in his conduct; neither pleased with idleness, nor too violently eager for employment. The routine of a university he seemed to continue when at court. He possessed more mirth of humour than of heart; he was a good companion, pliant, courteous, discreet, and able to forget and forgive an injury; yet never able to unite himself with those who overstept the limits of the right, the good, and the becoming.

GOETHE.

II.—THE KEY-NOTE TO HIS CHARACTER.

Figure to yourselves this youth, this son of princes; conceive him vividly, bring his state before your eyes, and then observe him when he learns that his father's spirit walks; stand by him in the terrors of the night, when the venerable ghost itself appears before him. A horrid shudder passes over him; he speaks to the mysterious form; he sees it beckon him; he follows it, and hears. The fearful accusation of his uncle rings in his ears; the summons to revenge; and the piercing, oft repeated prayer, "Remember me!"

And when the ghost has vanished, who is it that stands before us? A young hero panting for vengeance? A prince by birth, rejoicing to be called to punish the usurper of his crown? No! trouble and astonishment take hold of the solitary young man; he grows bitter against smiling villains, swears that he will not forget the spirit, and concludes with the significant ejaculation—

> The time is out of joint! O cursèd spite
> That ever I was born to set it right!

In these words, I imagine, will be found the key to Hamlet's whole procedure. To me it is clear that Shakespeare meant, in the present case, to represent the effects of a great action laid upon a soul unfit for the performance of it. In this view, the whole piece seems to me to be composed. We have here an oak planted in a costly vase, fit only to receive lovely flowers within its bosom; the roots expand, the vase is shattered.

A lovely, pure, noble and most moral nature, without the strength of nerve which forms a hero, sinks beneath a burden which it cannot bear and must not cast away. All duties are holy for him; the present is too hard. Impossibilities have been required of him; not in themselves impossibilities, but such for him. He winds, and turns, and torments himself; he advances and recoils; is ever put in mind, ever puts himself in mind; at last does all but lose his purpose from his thoughts; yet still without recovering his peace of mind.

GOETHE.

In Hamlet he [Shakespeare] seems to have wished to exemplify the moral necessity of a due balance between our attention to the objects of our senses, and our meditation on the workings of our minds—an equilibrium between the real and the imaginary worlds. In Hamlet this balance is disturbed : his thoughts, and the images of his fancy, are far more vivid than his actual perceptions, and his very perceptions, instantly passing through the medium of his contemplations, acquire, as they pass, a form and a colour not naturally their own. Hence we see a great, an almost enormous, intellectual activity, and a proportionate aversion to real action consequent upon it, with all its symptoms and accompanying qualities. This character Shakespeare places in circumstances under which it is obliged to act on the spur of the moment. Hamlet is brave and careless of death ; but he vacillates from sensibility, and procrastinates from thought, and loses the power of action in the energy of resolve.

* * * * * * *

Anything finer than this conception and working out of a great character is merely impossible. Shakespeare wished to impress upon us the truth, that action is the chief end of existence, that no faculties of intellect, however brilliant, can be considered valuable, or, indeed, otherwise than as misfortunes, if they withdraw us from, or render us repugnant to, action, and lead us to think and think of doing, until the time has elapsed when we can do anything effectually. In enforcing this moral truth, Shakespeare has shown the fulness and force of his powers : all that is amiable and excellent in nature is combined in Hamlet, with the exception of one quality—he is a man living in meditation, called upon to act by every motive, human and divine ; but the great object of his life is defeated by continually resolving to do, yet doing nothing but resolve.

COLERIDGE.

With respect to Hamlet's character, I cannot, as I understand the poet's views, pronounce altogether so favourable a sentence upon it as Goethe does. He is, it is true, of a highly cultivated mind, a prince of royal manners, endowed with the finest sense of propriety, susceptible of noble ambition, and open in the highest degree to an enthusiastic admiration of that excellence in others of which he himself is deficient. He acts the part of madness with unrivalled power, convincing the persons who are sent to examine into his supposed loss of reason, merely by telling them unwelcome truths, and rallying them with the most caustic wit. But in the resolutions which he so often embraces and always leaves unexecuted, his weakness is too apparent ; he does himself only justice when he implies that there is no greater dissimilarity than between himself and Hercules. He is not solely impelled by necessity to artifice and dissimulation, he has a natural inclination for crooked ways ; he is a hypocrite towards himself ; his far-fetched scruples are often mere pretexts to cover his want of determination : thoughts, as he says on a different occasion, which have

> But one part wisdom
> And ever three parts coward.

He has been chiefly condemned both for his harshness in repulsing the love of Ophelia, which he himself had cherished, and for his insensibility at her death. But he is too much overwhelmed with his own sorrow to have any compassion to spare for others ; besides, his outward indifference gives us by no means the measure of his internal perturbation. On the other hand, we evidently perceive in him a malicious joy, when he has succeeded in getting rid of his enemies, more through necessity and accident, which alone are able to impel him to quick and decisive measures, than by the merit of his own courage, as he himself confesses after the murder of Polonius, and with respect to Rosencrantz and Guildenstern. Hamlet has no firm belief either in himself or in anything else : from expressions of religious confidence he passes over to sceptical doubts ; he believes in the ghost of his father as long as he sees it, but as soon as it has disappeared, it appears to him almost in the light of a deception. He has even gone so far as to say, "there is nothing either good or bad, but thinking makes it so ;" with him the poet loses himself here in labyrinths of thought, in which neither end nor beginning is discoverable. The stars themselves, from the course of events, afford no answer to the question so urgently proposed to them. A voice from another world, commissioned, it would appear, by heaven, demands vengeance for a monstrous enormity, and the demand remains without effect ; the criminals are, at last, punished, but, as it were, by an accidental blow, and not in the solemn way requisite to convey to the world a warning example of justice ; irresolute foresight, cunning treachery, and impetuous rage, hurry on to a common destruction; the less guilty and the innocent are equally involved in the general ruin. The destiny of humanity is there exhibited as a gigantic Sphinx, which threatens to precipitate into the abyss of scepticism all who are unable to solve her dreadful enigmas.

SCHLEGEL.

Hamlet's mind, which is as noble as it is strong and sterling, in fact, as great as it is possible for the human mind to become, struggles continually to acquire that sovereignty which is to maintain the mastery of thought over the will, over the course and formation of human life. And yet he does not succeed in attaining his aim ; he does not possess sufficient strength to control external circumstances ; his own weakness and hesitation—supported as they are by the force of highly unfavourable relations—drive him perpetually from his path; unforeseen events frustrate his plans. For, on the one hand, his mind, in spite of its depth, greatness, and power, is, nevertheless, still wholly biassed in the contradiction of self-possessed activity with blind impulses, of free thought with unfree passion, of a morally necessary resolve with an arbitrary, accidental inclination. He does not, as yet, by any means, stand upon that height of moral strength and firmness of character, of perfect self-control and self-knowledge, which is the first indispensable condition of that grand, ideal activity of which Hamlet has dreamt, and which continually floats before his soul. On the other hand, this aspiration in its one-sidedness, by wishing of its own supreme power to rule and form all life, surpasses the measure of human power, and borders upon that arrogant desire which would wish to rid itself of the guiding hand of history, and to be in action " like an angel," in apprehension " like a god." Man certainly ought not to pursue his path in life according to blind instinct, but according to free and conscious thought.

ULRICI.

III.—HIS ARTISTIC TEMPERAMENT.

Hamlet, as I think, is by nature of an artistic, or, if it be preferred, of a philosophical frame of mind. This is the general foundation of his character. Like all minds poetically disposed, like all persons with a lively interest for art and knowledge, for mental culture, we find in him an earnest, striving and profound mind, naturally given to meditation and reflection, combined with a quickly aroused feeling of excitability and imagination, a delicate, sensitive nature, and an elasticity of reflection which, in moments of excitement, carry him involuntarily beyond the object in question, beyond the goal at which he is aiming ; thus bringing things, which in reality stand in different relation to him, into his immediate proximity. Shakespeare places special emphasis upon Hamlet's taste and love for poetry, his intimate acquaintance with the dramatic poetry of his age ; his fine judgment in regard to the object of the drama and the art of its representation, is proved by his conversation with the players. Express emphasis is also placed upon Hamlet's aversion, anger, and contempt in regard to all untruth, hypocrisy, pretence, and falsehood, in regard to a smooth, varnished appearance, as well as regards all want of culture, uncouthness, and vulgarity ; in other words, the poet emphasizes in him that feeling for truth which is so closely connected with the feeling for beauty, and which every artist, poet, and critic must possess, because it is the fundamental condition of his work. Shakespeare expressly states that Hamlet has studied in Wittenberg, and that, although thirty years of age, he cherishes the hope of returning thither to continue his studies. He expressly remarks that Horatio, Hamlet's bosom friend, to whom he is deeply and sincerely attached, is a "scholar." Everywhere, on every page, and on every line, the poet continually reminds us of Hamlet's own lofty mental culture, his eminent intelligence, his clear judgment, the acuteness and profundity of his reflections on the nature of man, the object of life, and the problems of art and philosophy. And yet Hamlet is by nature neither artist, poet, nor philosopher ; for this he obviously lacks the specific talent. But in the fundamental elements of his nature he does possess the talent, the power, and, consequently, also the desire to work towards the attainment of something *great*, to work in accordance with his *own thoughts*, in that *independent creative* activity which lies above the manifold domains of practical life. The strong desire in *this* way to prove the nobility of his soul—which is enthusiastic for all that is good and beautiful—is the mainspring of his life, the clue to his aims and actions. This fundamental feature of his inner nature has, during his youth, perfectly corresponded with the development of his outward existence. Growing up under the eyes of a noble, royal father, and being the heir to a mighty realm, he, in the sure prospect of free, regal power, which comes nearest to his ideal of human power and dignity, such as is possible only to princes, has given himself up wholly to the inward bent of his mind. Not originally inclined to sadness and melancholy, he seems, in accordance with the very fortunate position of his external circumstances, to cherish a happy view of life, even though he always was observant, pensive, and of a reflective turn of mind. This is attested by his fondness of and natural turn for humour and wit, for sarcastic puns and points, which he has evidently taken pleasure in developing, and cannot suppress even in his deep grief at the heavy calamities that have suddenly come upon him and destroyed both his inner and his outward life ; it is now, however, expressed more in the form of deeply meditative, incisive humour.

ULRICI.

IV.—HIS DEEP MELANCHOLY.

Hamlet is disqualified for action by his excess of the reflective tendencies, and by his unstable will, which alternates between complete inactivity and fits of excited energy. Naturally sensitive, he receives a painful shock from the hasty second marriage of his mother; already the springs of faith and joy in his nature are embittered ; then follows the terrible discovery of his father's murder, with the injunction laid upon him to revenge the crime ; upon this, again, follow the repulses which he receives from Ophelia. A deep melancholy lays hold of his spirit, and all of life grows dark and sad to his vision. Although hating his father's murderer, he has little heart to push on his revenge. He is aware that he is suspected and surrounded by spies. Partly to baffle them, partly to create a veil behind which to seclude his true self, partly because his own moral nature is, indeed, deeply disordered, he assumes the part of one whose wits have gone astray. Except for one loyal friend, he is alone among enemies or supposed traitors. Ophelia he regards as no more loyal or honest to him than his mother had been to her dead husband. The ascertainment of Claudius's guilt by means of the play still leaves him incapable of the last decisive act of vengeance. Not so, however, with the king, who, now recognizing his foe in Hamlet, does not delay to dispatch him to a bloody death in England.

EDWARD DOWDEN.

V.—THE SOURCE OF HIS MELANCHOLY.

Under Shakespeare's treatment, Hamlet's madness becomes something altogether different from the obstinate premeditation or melancholy enthusiasm of a young prince of the Middle Ages, placed in a dangerous condition, and engaged in a dark design ; it is a grave and moral condition, a great malady of soul, which, at certain epochs and in certain states of society and manners, frequently attacks the most highly gifted and noblest of our species, and afflicts them with a disturbance of mind which sometimes borders very closely upon madness. The world is full of evil, and of all kinds of evil. What sufferings, crimes, and fatal, although innocent, errors! What general and private iniquities, both strikingly apparent and utterly unknown! What merits, either stifled or neglected, become lost to the public and a burden to their possessors! What falsehood, and coldness, and levity, and ingratitude, and forgetfulness, abound in the relations and feelings of men ! Life is so short, and yet so agitated, sometimes so burdensome, and sometimes so empty! The future is so obscure. So much darkness at the end of so many trials. In reference to those who only see this phase of the world and of human destiny, it is easy to understand why their mind becomes disturbed, why their heart fails them, and why a misanthropic melancholy becomes an habitual feeling, which plunges them by turns into irritation or doubt, into ironical contempt or utter prostration. . . . . Read the four great monologues in which the Prince of Denmark abandons himself to the reflective expression of his inmost feelings ; gather together from the whole play the passages in which he casually gives them utterance ; seek out and sum up that which is manifest and that which is hidden in all he thinks and says, and you will everywhere recognize the presence of the moral malady just described. Therein truly resides, much more than in his personal griefs and perils, the source of Hamlet's melancholy ; in this consists his fixed idea and his madness. . . . . In order to render the exhibition of so sombre a disease not only endurable but attractive, Shakespeare has endowed the sufferer himself with the gentlest and most alluring qualities. He has made Hamlet handsome, popular, generous, affectionate, and even tender.

GUIZOT.

VI.—HIS HUMANITY.

Hamlet is a name ; his speeches and sayings but the idle coinage of the poet's brain. What, then, are they not real? They are as real as our own thoughts. Their reality is in the reader's mind. It is *we* who are Hamlet. This play has a prophetic truth, which is above that of history. Whoever has become thoughtful and melancholy through his own mishaps or those of others; whoever has borne about with him the clouded brow of reflection, and thought himself too much in the sun; whoever has seen the golden lamp of day dimmed by envious mists rising in his own breast, and could find in the world before him only a dull blank, with nothing left remarkable in it; whoever has known " The pangs of despised love, the insolence of office, and the spurns which patient merit of the unworthy takes," he who has felt his mind sink within him, and sadness cling to his heart like a malady, who has had his hope blighted and his youth staggered by the apparitions of strange things ; who cannot be well at ease, while he sees evil hovering near him like a spectre; whose powers of action have been eaten up by thought, he to whom the universe seems infinite, and himself nothing ; whose bitterness of soul makes him careless of consequences, and who goes to a play as his best resource to shove off, to a second remove, the evils of life by a mock representation of them—this is the true Hamlet.

HAZLITT.

VII.—THE IMPERSONATOR OF HAMLET MUST POSSESS, IN HIMSELF, A PECULIAR QUALITY OF PERSONAL FASCINATION.

Hamlet is a poetic ideal. He is not an ancient Dane, fair, blue-eyed, yellow-haired, stout, and lymphatic ; but he is the sombre, dreamy, mysterious hero of a melancholy poem. The actor who would represent him aright must not go behind the tragedy in which he occurs, in quest of historic realities, but, dealing with an ideal subject, must treat it in an ideal manner, as far removed as possible from the plane of actual life. Interest in the Prince of Denmark is not, to a very considerable extent, inspired by the circumstances that surround him, or by his proceedings : it depends upon the quality of the man—the interior spirit and fragrance of his character—and upon the words in which that spirit is expressed. There is an element in Hamlet, no less elusive than beautiful, which lifts the mind to a sombre height, fills the heart with a nameless grief, and haunts the soul as with remembered music of a gentle voice that will speak no more. It might be called sorrowful grandeur, sad majesty, ineffable mournfulness, grief-stricken isolation, or patient spiritual anguish. Whatever called, the name might prove inapt and inadequate ; but the magical force of this attribute can never fail to be felt. Hamlet fascinates by his personality ; and the actor can only succeed in presenting him, who possesses, in himself, this peculiar quality of fascination. It is something that cannot be drawn from the library, nor poured from the flagon, nor bought in the shops. Hamlet is, essentially, spiritual. It is not enough, therefore, in the presentation of this part, that the actor should make it known that Hamlet's soul is haunted by supernatural powers : he must also make it felt that Hamlet possesses a soul such as it is possible for supernatural powers to haunt. At the beginning, and before his mind has been shocked and unsettled by the awful apparition of his father's spirit in arms, he is found deeply prone to sombre thought upon the nothingness of this world and the solemn mystery of the world beyond the grave. This mental drift does not flow from his student fancy, but is the spontaneous, passionate tendency of his nature : for in the first self-communing monologue that he utters he is revealed as having brooded on the expediency of suicide ; and not long afterwards he avows belief that the powers of hell have great control over spirits, like his own, which are melancholy and weak. The soul of Hamlet, then, must be felt to have been in its original essence and condition, before grief, shame, and terror arrived to burden and distract it, intensely sensitive to the miseries that are in this world ; to the fact that all the pomp in human life is nothing but an evanescent pageant, passing, on a thin tissue, over what Shakespeare himself has so finely called "the blind cave of eternal night ; " and to all the strange, vague influences, sometimes beautiful, sometimes terrible, that seem wafted out of the great unknown. Out of this high sensibility, coupled with the conditions into which he is born and with the miserable state into which he is forced by the crimes of his mother and his uncle and the visitation of his father's ghost, the whole man may be

F

deduced. He is a compound of spiritualized intellect, masculine strength, feminine softness, over-imaginative reason, lassitude of thought, autumnal gloom, lovable temperament, piteous, tear-freighted humour, princely grace of condition, brooding melancholy, the philosophic mind, and the deep heart. His nature is everything noble ; he is placed upon a pinnacle of earthly greatness ; he is afflicted with a grief that breaks his heart, and thereupon with a shock that disorders his mind ; he is charged with a solemn and dreadful duty, to the fulfilment of which his will is wholly inadequate ; he sees so widely and understands so dubiously the nature of things, in the universe of God, that his sense of moral responsibility is overwhelmed and his power of action completely arrested ; he thinks greatly, but to no purpose ; he wanders darkly in the borderland betwixt reason and madness, haunted now with sweet strains and majestic images of heaven, and now, with terrific, uncertain shapes of hell ; and so he drifts aimlessly, on a sea of misery, to the oblivion of death. This man is a class of a type of beings on the earth to whom life is a dream, all its surroundings too vast and awful for endurance, all its facts sad, action impossible, or fitful and fruitless, and of whom it never can be said that they are happy till the grass is growing upon their graves.

William Winter.

It must be the praise of a man, who shall possess a genius more than the art of acting, to personate Hamlet, the gallant, the philosophical, the melancholy Hamlet, that amiable inconsistent who talked when he should have acted and acted when he should not even have talked, who, with a bosom wrung with sensibility, was unfeeling, and, in his very passion for justice, unjust, who in his misery had leisure for ridicule, and in his revenge for benevolence, who in the most melancholy abstraction never lost the graces of mind or the elegancies of manner, natural in the midst of artifice and estimable in the midst of error.

LEIGH HUNT.

VIII.—ON SOME OTHER CHARACTERS IN "HAMLET."

Nothing can be more affecting or beautiful than the Queen's apostrophe to Ophelia on throwing the flowers into the grave—

> Sweets to the sweet, farewell.　　　　[*Scattering flowers.*
> I hop'd thou should'st have been my Hamlet's wife.
> I thought thy bride-bed to have deck'd, sweet maid,
> And not have strew'd thy grave.

Shakespeare was thoroughly a master of mixed motives of human character, and he here shows us the Queen, who was so criminal in other respects, not without sensibility and affection in other relations of life. Ophelia is a character almost too exquisitely touching to be dwelt upon. O rose of May, O flower too soon faded! Her love, her madness, her death, are described with the truest touches of tenderness and pathos. It is a character which nobody but Shakespeare could have drawn in the way that he has done, and to the conception of which there is not even the smallest approach, except in some of the old romantic ballads. Her brother, Laertes, is a character we do not like so well; he is too hot and choleric, and somewhat rhodomontade. Polonius is a perfect character of its kind; nor is there any foundation for the objections which have been made to the consistency of this part. It is said that he acts very foolishly and talks very sensibly. There is no inconsistency in that. Again, that he talks wisely at one time, and foolishly at another; that his advice to Laertes is very excellent, and his advice to the King and Queen on the subject of Hamlet's madness, very ridiculous. But he gives the one as a father, and is sincere in it; he gives the other as a mere courtier, a busybody, and is accordingly officious, garrulous, and impertinent. In short, Shakespeare has been accused of inconsistency in this and other characters, only because he has kept up the distinction which there is in nature, between the understandings and the moral habits of men, between the absurdity of their ideas and the absurdity of their motives. Polonius is not a fool, but he makes himself so; his folly, whether in his actions or speeches, comes under the head of impropriety of intention.

HAZLITT.

IX.—HISTORY OF THE PLAY.

The story of Hamlet, Prince of Denmark, was first told in Latin, in the "Historia Danica" of Saxo Grammaticus, the Danish historian, who lived A.D. 1150—1220, and wrote his work between 1180 and 1208. The earliest known edition of it is that of Paris, 1514. The story as it there appears was incorporated in Francis de Belleforest's "Histoires Tragiques," the earlier volumes of which contained translations from the Italian of Bandello, amongst them being the history of "Romeo and Juliet." The story of Hamlet first appears in the fifth volume of these histories, which was printed at Paris in 1570. The story was thence translated into English. The only existing edition of this translation is that of 1608, and is in the library of Trinity College, Cambridge. The title of the book is "The Hystorie of Hamblet. London: Imprinted by *Richard Bradocke* for *Thomas Pauier*, and are to be sold at his shop in Corne-hill, neere to the Royall Exchange, 1608." It is reprinted in Collier's "Shakespeare's Library," and extracts from it are given below. No doubt there were earlier editions than that of 1608, from which Shakespeare worked. How greatly he improved upon the original story the reader may see for himself.

The play was first acted in 1602. On July 26 of that year we find an entry made by James Roberts, the printer, in the registers of the Stationers' Company, of "A Booke, The Revenge of Hamlett prince [of] Denmarke, as yt latelie was acted by the Lord Chamberlayne, his servantes." This is evidently the book that was printed in the following year under this title : "The Tragicall Historie of Hamlet Prince of Denmarke, by William Shakespeare. As it hath been diverse times acted by his Highnesse servantes in the Cittie of London : as also in the two Universities of Cambridge and Oxford, and else-where. At London printed for N. L. and John Trundell, 1603." Roberts probably printed this quarto as well as that of 1604, which was "Printed by I. R. for N. L."— that is, by James Roberts for Nicholas Ling. The last-mentioned edition of the play is the first genuine one. It first appeared as "The Tragicall Historie of Hamlet, Prince of Denmark. By William Shakespeare. Newly imprinted and enlarged to almost as much-againe as it was, according to the true and perfect coppie." The statement as to the enlargement of the play is substantially correct, for whereas the spurious edition of 1603 contained thirty-two leaves, the 1604 one had fifty, exclusive of the title. The edition of 1604 was followed by other quartos in 1605, 1611, 1637, and by one without date, but evidently printed from that of 1611. The folio of 1623, issued under the direction of Shakespeare's fellow-players, John Heminge and Henry Condell, was from a source independent of the quartos. Mr. Knight gave it as his opinion that, " All things considered, there never was a book so correctly printed as the first folio of Shakespeare." Messrs. Simpkin, Marshall & Co. have recently published, in a handy form, an accurate reprint of the first folio of Shakespeare's " Hamlet."

X.—" THE HYSTORIE OF HAMELET."

Fengon, having secretly assembled certain men, and perceiving himself strong enough to execute his enterprise—Horvendile, his brother, being at a banquet with his friends—suddenly set upon him, where he slew him as traitorously as cunningly he purged himself of so detestable a murder to his subjects ; for that before he had any violent or bloody hands, or once committed parricide upon his brother, he had incestuously abused his wife, whose honour he ought to have sought and procured, as traitorously he pursued and affected his destruction. . . . .

Boldened and encouraged by his impunity, Fengon ventured to couple himself in marriage with her . . . . and the unfortunate and wicked woman, that had the honour to be the wife of one of the valiantest and wisest princes of the north, imbased herself in such vile sort as to falsify her faith unto him, and, which is worse, to marry him that had been the tyrannous murderer of her lawful husband. . . . .

Geruth having so much forgotten herself, the prince Hamblet, perceiving himself to be in danger of his life, as being abandoned of his own mother, to beguile the tyrant into his subtleties, counterfeited the madman with such craft and subtle practices that he made show as if he had utterly lost his wits ; and under that vail he covered his pretence, and defended his life from the treasons and practices of the tyrant, his uncle.

For, every day being in the queen's palace (who as then was more careful to please her paramour, than ready to revenge the cruel death of her husband, or to restore her son to his inheritance), he rent and tore his clothes, wallowing and lying in the dirt and mire, running through the streets like a man distraught, not speaking one word but such as seemed to proceed of madness and mere frenzy; all his actions and gestures being no other than the right countenances of a man wholly deprived of all reason and understanding, in such sort, that as then he seemed fit for nothing but to make sport to the pages and ruffling courtiers that attended in the court of his uncle and father-in-law. But many times he did divers actions of great and deep consideration, and often made such and so fit answers, that a wise man would soon have judged from what spirit so fine an invention might proceed. . . . .

Hamblet likewise had intelligence of in what danger he was like to fall, if by any means he seemed to obey, or once like the wanton toys and vicious provocations of the gentlewoman sent to him by his uncle; which much abashed the prince, as then wholly being in affection to the lady; but by her he was likewise informed of the treason, as being one that from her infancy loved and favoured him, and would have been exceeding sorrowful for his misfortune. . . . .

Among the friends of Fengon there was one that, above all the rest, doubted of Hamblet's practices in counterfeiting the madman. His device to entrap Hamblet in his subtleties was this—that King Fengon should make as though he were to go some long voyage concerning affairs of great importance, and that, in the meantime, Hamblet should be shut up alone in a chamber with his mother, wherein some other should be secretly hidden behind the hangings; there to stand and hear their speeches, and the complots by them to be taken concern-

ing the accomplishment of the dissembling fool's pretence ;
. . . . and withal offered himself to be the man that
should stand to hearken and bear witness of Hamblet's speech
with his mother. . . . . This invention pleased the King
exceedingly well. . . . .

Meantime, the counsellor entered secretly into the Queen's
chamber, and there hid himself behind the arras, not long
before the Queen and Hamblet came thither, who, being crafty
and politic, as soon as he was in the chamber, doubting some
treason, used his ordinary manner of dissimulation, and began
to come, like a cock (beating with his arms in such manner
as cocks use to strike with their wings) upon the hangings of
the chamber, whereby, feeling something stirring under them,
he cried "A rat! a rat!" and, presently drawing his sword,
thrust it into the hangings, which done, he pulled the counsellor,
half dead, out by the heels, and made an end of killing
him. . . . . By which means having discovered the ambush,
and given the inventor thereof his just reward, he came again
to his mother, who in the meantime wept and tormented herself ;
and having once again searched every corner of the chamber,
perceiving himself to be alone with her, he began in sober
earnest and discreet manner to speak unto her, saying,

"What treason is this, O most infamous woman . . . .
who, under the veil of a dissembling creature, covereth the
most wicked and detestable crime that man could ever imagine
or was committed ? Now may I be assured to trust you, that
like a vile, wanton adultress, altogether impudent and given
over to her pleasure, runs spreading forth her arms to embrace
the traitorous, villainous tyrant that murdered my father ? . . . .
O, Queen Geruth ! it is licentiousness only that has made you
deface out of your mind the memory of the valour and virtues
of the good king, your husband and my father. . . . . Be

not offended, I pray you, madam, if, transported with dolour and grief, I speak so boldly unto you, and that I respect you less than duty requireth; for you, having forgotten me, and wholly rejected the memory of the deceased king, my father, must not be ashamed if I also surpass the bounds and limits of due consideration."

Although the Queen perceived herself nearly touched, and that Hamblet moved her to the quick, where she felt herself interested, nevertheless she forgot all disdain and wrath, which thereby she might have then have had, hearing herself so sharply chidden and reproved, to behold the gallant spirit of her son, and to think what she might hope, and the easier expect of his so great policy and wisdom. But on the one side, she durst not lift up her head to behold him, remembering her offence, and, on the other side, she would gladly have embraced her son, in regard of the wise admonitions given by him unto her. . . . .

After this, Fengon came to the court again, and determined that Hamblet must be sent into England. Now to bear him company were assigned two of Fengon's faithful ministers, bearing letters engraved in wood, containing Hamblet's death, in such sort as had advertised the King of England. But the subtle Danish prince, while his companions slept, having read the letters, and knowing his uncle's great treason, with the wicked and villainous minds of the two courtiers that led him to the slaughter, erased out the letters that concerned his death, and instead thereof graved others, with commission to the King of England to hang his two companions. . . . .

Hamblet, while his father lived, had been instructed in that devilish art, whereby the wicked spirit abuseth mankind, and advertiseth him of things past. It toucheth not the matter herein to discover whether this prince, by reason of his over-

G

great melancholy, had received those impressions, divining that which never any but himself had before declared. [Finally, the Hamblet of the "Hystorie" obtains a complete revenge, becomes King of Denmark, is twice married, and dies in battle.]

XI.—The Plan of "Hamlet."

The hero is without a plan, but the piece is full of plan. Here we have no villain punished on some self-conceived and rigidly-accomplished scheme of vengeance : a horrid deed occurs ; it rolls itself along with all its consequences, dragging guiltless persons also into its course ; the perpetrator seems as if he would evade the abyss which is made ready for him ; yet he plunges in, at the very point by which he thinks he shall escape and happily complete his course.

GOETHE.

THE END.